Volunteering to Help Seniors

Patrick Newell

Houston I.S.D.

Chavez High School Library
8501 Howard Drive
Houston, TX 77017

HIGH
interest
books

Children's Press
A Division of Grolier Publishing
New York / London / Hong Kong / Sydney
Danbury, Connecticut

Contributing Editor: Rob Kirkpatrick
Book Design: Michael DeLisio

Photo Credits: Cover, p. 4, 7, 8, 13, 14, 16, 18, 21, 22, 28, 33, 34, 41 ©
Indexstock; p. 10 © Robert Maass/Corbis; p. 24 © Pablo Corral V/Corbis;
p. 27 © Kelly-Mooney Photography/Corbis; p. 31 © Bob Rowan, Progressive
Image/Corbis; p. 37 © FPG; p. 38 © Kevin Fleming/Corbis

Visit Children's Press on the Internet at:
http://publishing.grolier.com

Cataloging-in-Publication Data

Newell, Patrick.
    Volunteering to help seniors / by Patrick Newell.
      p. cm. – (Service Learning)
    Includes bibliographical references and index.
    Summary: This book explains what service learning is,
gives examples of service-learning programs that help senior
citizens, and describes the benefits received by both seniors
and volunteers.
    ISBN 0-516-23399-8 (lib.bdg.) – ISBN 0-516-23577-X (pbk.)
    1. Voluntarism—United States—Juvenile literature
    2. Child volunteers—United States—Juvenile literature
    3. Young volunteers—United States—Juvenile literature
    4. Aged-Services for—United States—Juvenile literature
    [1. Voluntarism 2. Old age] I. Title. II. Series.
    HN90.V64 N48 2000   00-029460
    361.3'7'08350973—dc21

CONTENTS

INTRODUCTION

Debra was having trouble in school. She didn't get along with her teachers or classmates. She always acted tough, as if she had no cares in the world. But Debra was very insecure. She was uncomfortable around other people. She thought that she had no special talents or abilities.

Then, Debra joined a service-learning program. It was a program in which students met with senior citizens one-on-one. Debra went to a nursing home and made a senior friend. Her name was Lucy. Once a week, Debra went to visit Lucy. At first, Lucy would stay in a chair in the corner. She was like Debra—uncomfortable around other people.

Debra was having trouble in school. . .
until she made a senior friend.

5

But Debra sat by Lucy and talked to her. She got to know Lucy more and more each time. On Debra's fifth visit, she finally got Lucy to leave her chair and join in a group activity in the middle of the room. At the end of the day, Lucy hugged Debra. Lucy was happy to have someone there for her.

Debra was also happy. When she went to school the next day, she was friendly to her classmates. She answered her teacher's questions. Helping Lucy made Debra feel good about herself, which made her more outgoing.

Service-learning programs give students the chance to help seniors have better lives. These programs also help the service learners. Read on to find out more about the benefits that service learning can bring!

Service learning helped both Debra and her senior friend.

CHAPTER ONE

WHAT IS SERVICE LEARNING?

A volunteer is a person who works for the good of the community for no pay. People volunteer to make a positive change and to feel good about themselves. Volunteering is important. People find opportunities to volunteer through community organizations, churches, or private organizations.

Service learning is a form of volunteering. The difference between service learning and other volunteer work is that the volunteer gets special training and experience through service learning. For example, a service learner might gain organizational experience by being part of a team that creates its own

Working with seniors can be a positive service-learning experience.

Service learning projects teach valuable skills that you can use in the future.

project. Sometimes, volunteers in service-learning projects even can gain school credit.

BENEFITS TO THE COMMUNITY
Service-learning projects can make positive changes in communities. These projects can address many problems. Environmental pro-

grams can help to clean up parks and rivers, fight erosion (wearing away of ground soil), and plant trees. Programs to help the homeless might include collecting food, working at a homeless shelter, and educating the public. Senior citizens that have day-to-day problems also can benefit from student service learners. Service-learning projects can improve the community in many ways.

BENEFITS TO THE VOLUNTEER

Service-learning projects can make positive changes for the volunteer. As you work on a service-learning project, you will develop communication skills, leadership skills, and organizational skills. Working on a service-learning project will help you to develop these skills. Developing these skills will help you when it comes time to look for a job. Employers look for people who know how to communicate ideas, lead people, and organize tasks.

School Credit

In addition to new skills, you also may gain school credit for a service-learning project. In some places, schools require students to do service learning. Helping seniors is a great way to fulfill this requirement. If your school does not have a service-learning requirement, you still might be able to get extra credit for a service-learning project. Ask your favorite teacher or counselor about service-learning work.

Feeling Better About Yourself

Service learning also helps you to feel better about yourself. It feels good to help other people. You will come away knowing that you can make a difference in people's lives.

HELPING SENIORS

Elderly people often are forgotten in our society. Sometimes, injury or sickness keeps them homebound (unable to leave their

*Helping a homebound senior can
be a great service-learning project.*

houses). It is difficult for them to make and keep friends. Also, they may be unable to do home repairs. Their roofs may leak or the floorboards and stairways may become unsafe. These seniors need help in their homes.

Some elderly people live in places where they can receive daily medical care. These places are called nursing homes. Nursing

Volunteering in a place where seniors live can help them feel less lonely.

homes are positive places, but often the residents become lonely. Service learners can help them to feel less lonely.

Service-learning projects that help seniors are designed to make seniors' lives more comfortable and happy. But don't forget the other purpose of service learning. While the senior citizens you help will be getting many benefits, so will you.

Making Friends and Becoming a Leader

Take the example of Jose, a young boy who lives in Boston. Before he joined a service-learning program, he had few friends. No one had ever asked him to help out. He had never felt needed.

All of this changed when Jose joined a service-learning project to help seniors. He made new friends at the nursing home. After the first day, he felt close to the people there. He even hugged them good-bye. Jose became a leader in the program. He helped other students to befriend the seniors. Jose kept a journal of his experiences. He wrote of the fun times he was having with his new friends.

Jose's principal visited the nursing home to see how her students were doing. She was surprised to see that Jose was a leader. She told the adult group leader that Jose was not as outgoing in school. The group leader said Jose was definitely a leader in their service-learning project.

*Interacting with a senior can help
you become a more outgoing person.*

GIVING AND LEARNING

From Jose's example, we can see the entire purpose of service learning. The elderly folks found a new friend in Jose. He truly cared about them and wanted to spend time with them. They felt less lonely. At the same time, Jose showed leadership and communication skills which he would not display at school. Jose found a place where he belonged, and he became a more confident person. He felt good about himself, and his senior citizen friends were proud of him.

Learning Good Habits

When students join service-learning projects that help seniors, they can improve their own lives, too. Many of the skills used for a service-learning project also will be useful in school. For example, a project in Edgewood, Maryland, involved students who'd had trouble in school. They visited homebound elderly people and did chores around these people's homes. Many of these students had missed classes or done poorly with schoolwork. Once they became involved in the program for seniors, most students developed better habits. They came to school more often and behaved better in class. Their service-learning

FAST FACT

From 1984 to 1997, the number of high-school students participating in service learning rose from 81,000 to 2,967,262 per year. As of 1997, almost 2.5 million middle-school students also were doing service learning.

work had taught them how to budget their time. It also had made them feel part of a team, and had made them care more about their own lives.

CHAPTER TWO

FINDING SERVICE-LEARNING PROGRAMS

Helping seniors is a growing field in service learning. Why? The number of elderly people in our country keeps increasing. Better medicine and other medical treatments help people to live longer now than ever before. Also, a lot of babies were born in the twenty years after World War II (1939–1945). This time is called the baby boom. The children of the baby boom soon will become elderly people themselves. There will be more and more seniors in our society who need the help of younger people.

To find a service-learning program that works with seniors, try a number of places.

Many baby boomers will be seniors who need the help of younger people.

Look for programs at school, with community groups, or with government organizations.

SERVICE LEARNING AT YOUR SCHOOL

The first place to look for a service-learning opportunity is at your school. For example, in Belmont, Massachusetts, the Belmont Hill School sponsors two separate service-learning opportunities for its students. One project asks students to do minor chores and work projects around the homes of local elderly folks. These chores include doing yard work, moving furniture, and cleaning. The other part of the project asks students to visit local elderly citizens. They visit during school time in the morning as part of their school program. A local restaurant donates pastries for the students to take. The students and the seniors are together for forty minutes a day. As an added benefit, the seniors also are invited to free showings of school plays.

Some schools have service-learning programs that encourage students to visit seniors in their homes.

COMMUNITY GROUPS

Another place to look for service-learning opportunities is through community groups such as youth groups or churches. In one 4-H sponsored project in Stephenson, Michigan, young people help homebound senior citizens. This project allows the primary caregiver (live-in nurse) a chance to leave the house. Nurses train these volunteers in many

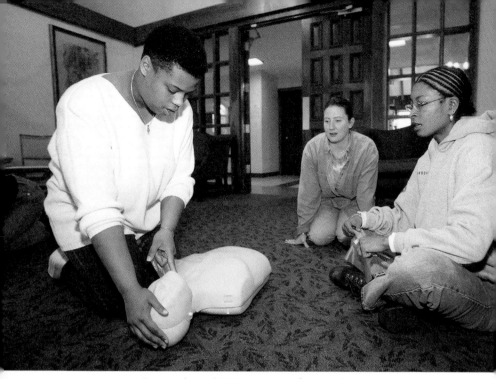

Learning CPR can teach you how to
help a senior in case of an emergency.

skills, including first aid and what to do in an emergency. The students become friends with homebound senior citizens so that the older people feel less cut off from society.

GOVERNMENT PROGRAMS

Another place to find service-learning opportunities is through a government-sponsored activity. State colleges or universities sponsor many activities. Some counties or cities have departments that deal with issues relating to elderly people. In Olathe, Kansas, the Johnson County Human Resources and Aging Department trains volunteers to help seniors. Volunteers learn how to talk to and listen to elderly people. They learn what to do in case of an emergency. They work with the medical staff to report any changes in their friends' conditions. Also, the volunteers help to raise money to fund the project.

FAST FACT

Approximately 53 per-cent of all high-school service learners are female.

HELPING IN DIFFERENT WAYS

You may have noticed there are two types of projects. The first type deals with a one-on-one friendship with a senior citizen. The other type uses a team to help many seniors at once in the community. Read on to find out more about both types.

CHAPTER THREE

ONE ON ONE

Are you interested in making a new friend? Your first task is to find a program that will support you. You will need training and people to talk to about your experiences. The best place to start looking is at your school. Your school may offer service-learning programs that you can join. If not, a teacher or counselor can help you locate one. At the end of this book, there is a list of books and Web sites you can use to find a project in your area.

Once you have found a project that you would like to participate in, the next step is to meet your project coordinator. In many

Your service-learning counselor can give you helpful advice.

programs, this person is an adult. This person's job is to coordinate the volunteers and listen to their suggestions. He or she also is there to arrange for the most important part of service learning. This is the training during which you will find out how to do your job in the best way you can.

The first aspect of the training usually discusses the myths (false beliefs) and facts about older people. At first, you may be afraid to meet someone who is different than you are. This training will help you to learn more about interacting with seniors. Then, you will have an idea of what to expect.

Before you meet your new friend, you will learn how to communicate with seniors. You will learn how to listen. For example, when you listen, you should sit with your arms and legs uncrossed. This keeps you from looking impatient or bored. You also will learn how to ask questions.

*Your service-learning training will
teach you how to interact with seniors.*

Volunteers need to know emergency skills when dealing with senior citizens. You may have to give the Heimlich maneuver if your senior starts choking on food. Some elderly folks need help moving around. You will learn how to help them. Finally, some senior citizens have physical or medical needs that you will need to know

You can help a senior plan a healthy diet.

how to handle. You may even have to help them to balance their diets, or to fill out paperwork for their government benefits.

You will be trained a great deal before you even meet your friend. Once you have been visiting your friend for awhile, you still should meet other volunteers and discuss your experiences. You also should get on-going training to answer questions that come up in your visits.

You have joined a project, received training, and found a friend. What do you do now? It is time to do some activities with your new friend. Many projects have set activities already planned for you. However, you and your friend are not bound by them. This is where your new communication and interview skills come into play. Some seniors would just like a chance to go outside. Some just want someone to talk to them. Once you know your new friend, you will find things you both like to do. That's what friends are for.

MAGIC ME

Boston has a service-learning program called Magic Me. The Magic Me program has four parts. The first is service. This is the work the volunteers do when they are with their friends. They do activities that include physical exercise, art projects, and storytelling.

The next part of this program is reflection. Volunteers write a journal of what happens to them. All of the volunteers meet once a month to share information and stories.

The third part of the program deals with the future of the volunteer. This part explores what the volunteer has learned. It also helps to show the volunteer what he or she can do in the future with the skills and experiences gained in a service-learning project. A volunteer learns better communication skills. He or she may have learned how to resolve conflicts. This part of the program also can help a volunteer to explore career choices.

The final part of the Magic Me program is spent learning leadership skills. The volunteers spend one day at a leadership workshop. In this workshop, the students work to improve the Magic Me program. They also learn to work together.

A MUSICAL FRIENDSHIP

A service learner named Bobby discovered something new about his blind friend Mary. Bobby found out through talking with his new friend that she plays the piano. None of

Encouraging the elderly to pursue their musical talents can help them to better enjoy their lives.

the nurses knew this, even though she had been in the nursing home for many years. Bobby and the residents received a wonderful concert. Bobby had been a kid who liked to fight. Once he met Mary, he began to settle down. Being with Mary gave him confidence in himself. Mary was no longer lonely. She found that she could still please people with music. Bobby found that he could reach people. He could be noticed without having to fight.

One-on-one projects such as Bobby's are a great way to help seniors. You also can help yourself. When you talk to a senior, he or she can share memories and stories. This helps him or her to feel important and less lonely. Also, you have the chance to learn from seniors' experiences. Old people can be very wise. One-on-one service learning helps you to benefit from a senior's wisdom.

FAST FACT

A 1997 poll found that 80 percent of service-learning students got an A or B grade average in school.

A LITTLE PATIENCE

When you talk to a senior, you must remember to be patient. Seniors sometimes have trouble hearing. Sometimes they have trouble remembering things. This does not mean that they are stupid. It just means they need someone to speak clearly to them. If your senior friend does not hear what you

It helps to show patience and understanding when working with seniors.

say, simply repeat your question or comment. If a senior repeats himself or herself, do not act annoyed. When working with seniors, a little patience goes a long way.

CHAPTER FOUR

GROUP PROJECTS THAT HELP SENIORS

Some people like to work in groups. They may feel shy about working one-on-one. That's okay. Service learners do not have to work one-on-one to help seniors. There are many group projects with seniors on which service learners may work.

Just as with one-on-one service learning, you will need to locate a sponsor. Again, your school is a good place to look first. Your teachers, principal, or guidance counselor can tell you about opportunities at school. If there are none, you can find community projects to join.

Once you have a sponsor or a group to work with, the next step is to decide what

Group projects, such as a food distribution campaign, can help the elderly, too.

sort of project you would like to do. What do senior citizens in your area need? How can your group help? Can seniors in your neighborhood get food during snowstorms? Are their sidewalks clean and safe? Do they need someone to check in on them?

Some groups have been doing the same project for a long time. If this is the case, they will welcome your new ideas. If they are starting a brand-new project, you can help them to plan it.

Once you decide on a group project, you need to plan it. You need to discuss how each part of the project will get done. Who will be responsible for which tasks? What special skills does each person have? Who will be in charge of the group?

GETTING PERMISSION
After you plan out exactly what needs to happen, you need to get permission to do the project you want. If you are building some-

Talk with your parent or guardian before committing to a service-learning project.

thing, you will need the permission of the town, county, or city to allow for a building permit. If you plan on helping a nursing home by planting flowerbeds or arranging to take all of the residents to a play, you will need the permission of the nursing home. Also, you need to get permission from a parent or guardian for every service-learning student.

Groups can raise funds through
programs such as benefit dinners.

ADVERTISING YOUR GROUP PROJECT

Once your group has the permission it needs, you may need to advertise, or make the public aware of what you want to do. You can do many things by advertising your project. You can get people to donate any materials you might need. You can get other students to join your group. Advertising also can help you to raise money.

FUND-RAISING

Does your project require money? Even if you are only putting on a play at a nursing home, you may need to pay for props and costumes. If you are replacing the roofs on the homes of the elderly, you will need a great deal of money. Getting money for a project is called fund-raising. Knowing how to raise funds takes a lot of training. You have to tell the donor, or the person who may give money, what it is you are doing. You need to explain how it will benefit seniors and the communi-

Teen Team to the Rescue

In Camden, Maine, a community-service project works to improve the housing of local seniors. These people have neither the extra money nor the physical abilities to fix their own homes. Teenagers of the Camden area who volunteer are taught home-repair skills. They build wheelchair ramps. They weatherize the homes of the elderly (making the buildings warmer in the winter and cooler in the summer). They also paint houses and do any small repairs that are needed. Adults who have construction experience supervise the volunteers.

ty. You need to tell the donor how his help will make a difference. Fund-raising can be hard to do. You may need an adult to help you.

A WIN-WIN SITUATION

No matter which type of service-learning project you work on, you can learn a lot from service-learning work with seniors. If you visit a special friend, you will learn how to communicate and how to listen. If you choose to help an entire community of senior citizens, you will practice your organization and leadership skills. Either way, you may earn credit for school or gain experience for later in life.

You will gain a great deal by doing service-learning projects with seniors. Seniors also can benefit greatly from your service-learning work, whether you become a senior's friend, fix his home, or deliver groceries. Yvonne, a service learner in Boston, said, "I like it when I am able to get someone to smile."

Service work with seniors can help you become a better person.

advertising using posters, commercials, phone calls or other methods to make the public aware of a service-learning project

donor a person who gives money or materials to help complete a project

erosion the wearing away of soil

fund-raising convincing citizens, businesses, or government agencies to give money to support a service-learning project

Heimlich maneuver a skill used to help someone who is choking

homebound when someone cannot leave his or her home because of sickness or old age

leadership skills the ability to have people follow you when trying to complete a project

myth a false belief

organizational skills skills a person learns
to help put together projects and make
the project work in the best and simplest
way

primary caregiver a nurse or family mem-
ber that helps a sick or elderly person
most of the time in doing that person's
daily tasks

weatherize to make a building warm in the
winter and cool in the summer

Branson, Richard. *Worldwide Volunteering for Young People 2000.* London: Youth for Britain, 2000.

Erlbach, Arlene. *The Kids' Volunteering Book.* New York: Lerner Publishing Group,1998.

Hovanec, Erin M. *Get Involved! A Girl's Guide to Volunteering.* New York: Rosen Publishing Group,1999.

Lewis, Barbara A. *The Kid's Guide to Service Projects.* New York: Free Spirit Press, 1996.

ORGANIZATIONS

American Red Cross
Attn: Public Inquiry Office
431 18th Street, NW
Washington, D.C. 20006

National Council for Senior Citizens
1331 F Street, NW
Washington D.C. 20004
(202) 347-8800

National 4-H Council
7100 Connecticut Avenue
Chevy Chase, MD 20815
(301) 961-2800
Web site: *www.fourhcouncil.edu*

WEB SITES

Are You Into It
www.areyouintoit.com
This site talks about volunteer activities in the 4-H. There is a place to write your own volunteering experiences. This site includes many links to local 4-H groups and to other volunteering sites.

KidsHealth.org – Hey Teens
http://kidshealth.org/teen
This site is a general resource for teens. It includes a teen guide to volunteering, ideas for projects, and ways to become involved.

INDEX

INDEX

ABOUT THE AUTHOR

Patrick C. Newell has done a great deal of volunteer work through his involvement in the Boy Scouts. He is an Eagle Scout. He currently resides in Chicago, Illinois, where he attends Columbia College and is pursuing an MFA in creative writing.

DATE DUE			
MAY 10 2005